The Scope

Success worth billions was once an idea. It is so important to hold our own ideas with infinite value even if our current situations don't reflect prosperity. Not every idea will pan out the way entrepreneurs hope but only one is required for a full change of future outlook.

-

Completing exercises for all five business ideas may reveal one in particular that stands about above the rest. Respect the journey and give your ideas a fighting chance!

-

The instructions are simple. Fill out the exercises with what comes to mind. Keep your notes close because ideas aren't the most well behaved in terms of timing, for example, 3:48AM. If you have purchased these exercises, you likely have some business ideas to expand on. This book holds twenty exercises for five different business ideas (likely ones you have selected above the rest). When complete, pay close attention on which of your ideas feel the most right.

"

SHORT MISSION STATEMENT OR SUMMARY

The Powerhouse of WHY

Identify 10 short, dynamite reasons why your business absolutely must be in existence. Arm yourself with reasoning and why you want this idea fulfilled. These statements may be used later on to present to stakeholders and customers.

Invisible Assets

List networks, equipment, software and anything you may already have access to that other people may not commonly have. This list can be ongoing as some assets to be grateful for may not come to mind right away.

Design 3 Logos

1. Incorporate an object 2. Create a logo with related symbolism to your mission statement 3. Create a logo after having looked at 5 logos from competition. Which one of your 3 designs stands out to you?

Plan to Give

Indicate a target of when you would decide to give
to a charity, visualize what it would be?
What charities are related to your business model?

Be Prepared

List important dates and ideas complimenting those dates for events and themes. Examples: -Community events -National Days -Fundraisers -Unique holidays How can these dates benefit your business?

____

____

____

____

____

____

____

____

____

____

____

____

____

____

____

____

____

Design the overhead view of your ideal business work or sales space. If your proposed business idea does not include a physical sales or service floor, design what you envision the most efficient work set up would be for it.

Loose Ends

Identify three possible areas your business may fall short or behind in projections (sales, services or timelines) and create three solid strategies to combat those short falls.

Dreaded Expenses

List all expenses you can think of in five minutes and

brainstorm a way to make each one lower.

Within Your Capability

This brainstorm may require some bold thinking. List sources of unexpected income you could potentially receive with the skills, equipment and any other abilities you may possess.

If you have a planned location for your sales or work-space, identify three accessibility flaws (or areas that could be better) within that location. What are some ways to alleviate those accessibility issues for yourself, customers or future staff?

From The Future

Visualize that you are sitting down for a beverage of your choice with you ten years in the future that has been in successful business for that time. What advice do you think would be given during this conversation?

List all physical items that you may need to rent, purchase or pay a subscription for in the first five years. Compare physical items to the purchase price and answer questions like is it a product that needs frequent upgrading? With the product last a very long time? Does the asset include a warranty over 10 years?

Not only is going green or better for the environment but it tends to be much more appealing ever increasingly wise clientel. List five features of you business idea and come up with ways to make them environmentally friendly. If your business idea is already environment oriented, List the ways you make your business eco-friendly yet keep costs down.

Digital Delve

Layout what the front page of your website will look like and list all of the sub-sites it will include.

Using your "Powerhouse of WHY" answers, create a summarized mission statement that incorporates your personal goals as well as the ones in your idea. It is encouraged to recite this mission statement out loud twice in the morning and twice before you go to bed to keep your mission aligned.

Securing Cashflow

Research cashflow diagrams and create your own while incorperating the expenses you brainstormed in the expense exercise. Try to include feasible ways to combat your expenses by incorperating ideas from your unexpected sources of income exercise.

Invisible Competitors

Indicate three "invisible competitors" (meaning businesses that could compete with yours if they discovered the potential to.) What would still set you apart?

In earlier exercises you were asked to name thing like how you intend to combat a strong point of a competitive business or things that set you apart. This time, locate 3-5 competitors and indicate a mistake you think they are making with their business and how they could improve.

Three Mountains

Identify three major hurtles you expect within the start-up period and break down 3 gameplan steps for each hurtle to overcome them all.

Write down at least 7 steps from sucessful launch (at the top) to very start (at the bottom).

DAY OF LAUNCH! SUCCESS! TO DO:

**VERY BEGINNING STAGES
TO DO:**

Notes / Reflections / Take-aways

IDEA

#2

SHORT MISSION STATEMENT OR SUMMARY

The Powerhouse of WHY

Identify 10 short, dynamite reasons why your business absolutely must be in existence. Arm yourself with reasoning and why you want this idea fulfilled. These statements may be used later on to present to stakeholders and customers.

Invisible Assets

List networks, equipment, software and anything you may already have access to that other people may not commonly have. This list can be ongoing as some assets to be grateful for may not come to mind right away.

Design 3 Logos

1. Incorporate an object 2. Create a logo with related symbolism to your mission statement 3. Create a logo after having looked at 5 logos from competition. Which one of your 3 designs stands out to you?

Plan to Give

Indicate a target of when you would decide to give
to a charity, visualize what it would be?
What charities are related to your business model?

____

Be Prepared

List important dates and ideas complimenting those dates for events and themes. Examples: -Community events -National Days -Fundraisers -Unique holidays How can these dates benefit your business?

____

____

____

____

____

____

____

____

____

____

____

____

____

____

____

____

<u>Make Space Meaningful</u>

Design the overhead view of your ideal business work or sales space. If your proposed business idea does not include a physical sales or service floor, design what you envision the most efficient work set up would be for it.

Loose Ends

Identify three possible areas your business may fall short or behind in projections (sales, services or timelines) and create three solid strategies to combat those short falls.

Dreaded Expenses

List all expenses you can think of in five minutes and
brainstorm a way to make each one lower.

Within Your Capability

This brainstorm may require some bold thinking. List sources of unexpected income you could potentially receive with the skills, equipment and any other abilities you may possess.

Accessible

If you have a planned location for your sales or work-space, identify three accessibility flaws (or areas that could be better) within that location. What are some ways to alleviate those accessibility issues for yourself, customers or future staff?

From The Future

Visualize that you are sitting down for a beverage of your choice with you ten years in the future that has been in successful business for that time. What advice do you think would be given during this conversation?

List all physical items that you may need to rent, purchase or pay a subscription for in the first five years. Compare physical items to the purchase price and answer questions like is it a product that needs frequent upgrading? With the product last a very long time? Does the asset include a warranty over 10 years?

Not only is going green or better for the environment but it tends to be much more appealing ever increasingly wise clientel. List five features of you business idea and come up with ways to make them environmentally friendly. If your business idea is already environment oriented, List the ways you make your business eco-friendly yet keep costs down.

Digital Delve

Layout what the front page of your website will look like and list all of the sub-sites it will include.

Using your "Powerhouse of WHY" answers, create a summarized mission statement that incorporates your personal goals as well as the ones in your idea. It is encouraged to recite this mission statement out loud twice in the morning and twice before you go to bed to keep your mission aligned.

Securing Cashflow

Research cashflow diagrams and create your own while incorperating the expenses you brainstormed in the expense exercise. Try to include feasible ways to combat your expenses by incorperating ideas from your unexpected sources of income exercise.

Invisible Competitors

Indicate three "invisible competitors" (meaning businesses that could compete with yours if they discovered the potential to.) What would still set you apart?

<u>Mistakes to Avoid</u>

In earlier exercises you were asked to name thing like how you intend to combat a strong point of a competitive business or things that set you apart. This time, locate 3-5 competitors and indicate a mistake you think they are making with their business and how they could improve.

Three Mountains

Identify three major hurtles you expect within the <u>start-up period</u> and break down 3 gameplan steps for each hurtle to overcome them all.

Write down at least 7 steps from sucessful launch (at the top) to very start (at the bottom).

DAY OF LAUNCH! SUCCESS! TO DO:

VERY BEGINNING STAGES TO DO:

Notes / Reflections / Take-aways

45

IDEA

#3

SHORT MISSION STATEMENT OR SUMMARY

<u>The Powerhouse of WHY</u>

Identify 10 short, dynamite reasons why your business absolutely must be in existence. Arm yourself with reasoning and why you want this idea fulfilled. These statements may be used later on to present to stakeholders and customers.

Invisible Assets

List networks, equipment, software and anything you may already have access to that other people may not commonly have. This list can be ongoing as some assets to be grateful for may not come to mind right away.

Design 3 Logos

1. Incorporate an object 2. Create a logo with related symbolism to your mission statement 3. Create a logo after having looked at 5 logos from competition. Which one of your 3 designs stands out to you?

Plan to Give

Indicate a target of when you would decide to give
to a charity, visualize what it would be?
What charities are related to your business model?

Be Prepared

List important dates and ideas complimenting those dates for events and themes. Examples:
-Community events -National Days -Fundraisers -Unique holidays How can these dates benefit your business?

<u>Make Space Meaningful</u>

Design the overhead view of your ideal business work or sales space. If your proposed business idea does not include a physical sales or service floor, design what you envision the most efficient work set up would be for it.

Loose Ends

Identify three possible areas your business may fall short or behind in projections (sales, services or timelines) and create three solid strategies to combat those short falls.

Dreaded Expenses

List all expenses you can think of in five minutes and brainstorm a way to make each one lower.

Within Your Capability

This brainstorm may require some bold thinking. List sources of unexpected income you could potentially receive with the skills, equipment and any other abilities you may possess.

Accessible

If you have a planned location for your sales or work-space, identify three accessibility flaws (or areas that could be better) within that location. What are some ways to alleviate those accessibility issues for yourself, customers or future staff?

From The Future

Visualize that you are sitting down for a beverage of your choice with you ten years in the future that has been in successful business for that time. What advice do you think would be given during this conversation?

Buy or Rent?

List all physical items that you may need to rent, purchase or pay a subscription for in the first five years. Compare physical items to the purchase price and answer questions like is it a product that needs frequent upgrading? With the product last a very long time? Does the asset include a warranty over 10 years?

Not only is going green or better for the environment but it tends to be much more appealing ever increasingly wise clientel. List five features of you business idea and come up with ways to make them environmentally friendly. If your business idea is already environment oriented, List the ways you make your business eco-friendly yet keep costs down.

Digital Delve

Layout what the front page of your website will look like and list all of the sub-sites it will include.

Coming Together

Using your "Powerhouse of WHY" answers, create a summarized mission statement that incorporates your personal goals as well as the ones in your idea. It is encouraged to recite this mission statement out loud twice in the morning and twice before you go to bed to keep your mission aligned.

Securing Cashflow

Research cashflow diagrams and create your own while incorperating the expenses you brainstormed in the expense exercise. Try to include feasible ways to combat your expenses by incorperating ideas from your unexpected sources of income exercise.

Invisible Competitors

Indicate three "invisible competitors" (meaning businesses that could compete with yours if they discovered the potential to.) What would still set you apart?

Mistakes to Avoid

In earlier exercises you were asked to name thing like how you intend to combat a strong point of a competitive business or things that set you apart. This time, locate 3-5 competitors and indicate a mistake you think they are making with their business and how they could improve.

Three Mountains

Identify three major hurtles you expect within the start-up period and break down 3 gameplan steps for each hurtle to overcome them all.

Write down at least 7 steps from sucessful launch (at the top) to

very start (at the bottom).

DAY OF LAUNCH! SUCCESS! TO DO:

**VERY BEGINNING STAGES
TO DO:**

Notes / Reflections / Take-aways

IDEA #4

SHORT MISSION STATEMENT OR SUMMARY

<u>The Powerhouse of WHY</u>

Identify 10 short, dynamite reasons why your business absolutely must be in existence. Arm yourself with reasoning and why you want this idea fulfilled. These statements may be used later on to present to stakeholders and customers.

Invisible Assets

List networks, equipment, software and anything you may already have access to that other people may not commonly have. This list can be ongoing as some assets to be grateful for may not come to mind right away.

Design 3 Logos

1. Incorporate an object 2. Create a logo with related symbolism to your mission statement 3. Create a logo after having looked at 5 logos from competition. Which one of your 3 designs stands out to you?

Plan to Give

Indicate a target of when you would decide to give to a charity, visualize what it would be?
What charities are related to your business model?

Be Prepared

List important dates and ideas complimenting those dates for events and themes. Examples: -Community events -National Days -Fundraisers -Unique holidays How can these dates benefit your business?

<u>Make Space Meaningful</u>

Design the overhead view of your ideal business work or sales space. If your proposed business idea does not include a physical sales or service floor, design what you envision the most efficient work set up would be for it.

Loose Ends

Identify three possible areas your business may fall short or behind in projections (sales, services or timelines) and create three solid strategies to combat those short falls.

Dreaded Expenses

List all expenses you can think of in five minutes and
brainstorm a way to make each one lower.

Within Your Capability

This brainstorm may require some bold thinking. List sources of unexpected income you could potentially receive with the skills, equipment and any other abilities you may possess.

Accessible

If you have a planned location for your sales or work-space, identify three accessibility flaws (or areas that could be better) within that location. What are some ways to alleviate those accessibility issues for yourself, customers or future staff?

From The Future

Visualize that you are sitting down for a beverage of your choice with you ten years in the future that has been in successful business for that time. What advice do you think would be given during this conversation?

Buy or Rent?

List all physical items that you may need to rent, purchase or pay a subscription for in the first five years. Compare physical items to the purchase price and answer questions like is it a product that needs frequent upgrading? With the product last a very long time? Does the asset include a warranty over 10 years?

Not only is going green or better for the environment but it tends to be much more appealing ever increasingly wise clientel. List five features of you business idea and come up with ways to make them environmentally friendly. If your business idea is already environment oriented, List the ways you make your business eco-friendly yet keep costs down.

Digital Delve

Layout what the front page of your website will look like and list all of the sub-sites it will include.

Using your "Powerhouse of WHY" answers, create a summarized mission statement that incorporates your personal goals as well as the ones in your idea. It is encouraged to recite this mission statement out loud twice in the morning and twice before you go to bed to keep your mission aligned.

Securing Cashflow

Research cashflow diagrams and create your own while incorperating the expenses you brainstormed in the expense exercise. Try to include feasible ways to combat your expenses by incorperating ideas from your unexpected sources of income exercise.

Invisible Competitors

Indicate three "invisible competitors" (meaning businesses that could compete with yours if they discovered the potential to.) What would still set you apart?

In earlier exercises you were asked to name thing like how you intend to combat a strong point of a competitive business or things that set you apart. This time, locate 3-5 competitors and indicate a mistake you think they are making with their business and how they could improve.

Three Mountains

Identify three major hurtles you expect within the start-up period and break down 3 gameplan steps for each hurtle to overcome them all.

Reverse Engineer in Seven Steps or More

Write down at least 7 steps from sucessful launch (at the top) to

very start (at the bottom).

DAY OF LAUNCH! SUCCESS! TO DO:

**VERY BEGINNING STAGES
TO DO:**

Notes / Reflections / Take-aways

IDEA

#5

SHORT MISSION STATEMENT
OR SUMMARY

The Powerhouse of WHY

Identify 10 short, dynamite reasons why your business absolutely must be in existence. Arm yourself with reasoning and why you want this idea fulfilled. These statements may be used later on to present to stakeholders and customers.

Invisible Assets

List networks, equipment, software and anything you may already have access to that other people may not commonly have. This list can be ongoing as some assets to be grateful for may not come to mind right away.

Design 3 Logos

1. Incorporate an object 2. Create a logo with related symbolism to your mission statement 3. Create a logo after having looked at 5 logos from competition. Which one of your 3 designs stands out to you?

Plan to Give

Indicate a target of when you would decide to give to a charity, visualize what it would be?

What charities are related to your business model?

Be Prepared

List important dates and ideas complimenting those dates for events and themes. Examples: -Community events -National Days -Fundraisers -Unique holidays How can these dates benefit your business?

<u>Make Space Meaningful</u>

Design the overhead view of your ideal business work or sales space. If your proposed business idea does not include a physical sales or service floor, design what you envision the most efficient work set up would be for it.

Loose Ends

Identify three possible areas your business may fall short or behind in projections (sales, services or timelines) and create three solid strategies to combat those short falls.

Dreaded Expenses

List all expenses you can think of in five minutes and brainstorm a way to make each one lower.

Within Your Capability

This brainstorm may require some bold thinking.
List sources of unexpected income you could
potentially receive with the skills, equipment and any
other abilities you may possess.

Accessible

If you have a planned location for your sales or work-space, identify three accessibility flaws (or areas that could be better) within that location. What are some ways to alleviate those accessibility issues for yourself, customers or future staff?

Visualize that you are sitting down for a beverage of your choice with you ten years in the future that has been in successful business for that time. What advice do you think would be given during this conversation?

Buy or Rent?

List all physical items that you may need to rent, purchase or pay a subscription for in the first five years. Compare physical items to the purchase price and answer questions like is it a product that needs frequent upgrading? With the product last a very long time? Does the asset include a warranty over 10 years?

Not only is going green or better for the environment but it tends to be much more appealing ever increasingly wise clientel. List five features of you business idea and come up with ways to make them environmentally friendly. If your business idea is already environment oriented, List the ways you make your business eco-friendly yet keep costs down.

Digital Delve

Layout what the front page of your website will look like and list all of the sub-sites it will include.

Using your "Powerhouse of WHY" answers, create a summarized mission statement that incorporates your personal goals as well as the ones in your idea. It is encouraged to recite this mission statement out loud twice in the morning and twice before you go to bed to keep your mission aligned.

Securing Cashflow

Research cashflow diagrams and create your own while incorperating the expenses you brainstormed in the expense exercise. Try to include feasible ways to combat your expenses by incorperating ideas from your unexpected sources of income exercise.

Invisible Competitors

Indicate three "invisible competitors" (meaning businesses that could compete with yours if they discovered the potential to.) What would still set you apart?

____

____

____

____

____

____

____

____

____

____

____

____

____

____

In earlier exercises you were asked to name thing like how you intend to combat a strong point of a competitive business or things that set you apart. This time, locate 3-5 competitors and indicate a mistake you think they are making with their business and how they could improve.

Three Mountains

Identify three major hurtles you expect within the start-up period and break down 3 gameplan steps for each hurtle to overcome them all.

Write down at least 7 steps from sucessful launch (at the top) to

very start (at the bottom).

DAY OF LAUNCH! SUCCESS! TO DO:

VERY BEGINNING STAGES
        TO DO:

Notes / Reflections / Take-aways